Pearl Bailey

WITH A SONG IN HER HEART

by Keith Brandt
illustrated by Gershom Griffith

Troll Associates

Pearl Bailey

WITH A SONG IN HER HEART

Library of Congress Cataloging-in-Publication Data

Brandt, Keith, (date)
    Pearl Bailey: with a song in her heart / by Keith Brandt;
illustrated by Gershom Griffith.
      p.   cm.
    Summary: A biography of the singer who entertained audiences with
her performances on Broadway, television, and the concert stage.
    ISBN 0-8167-2921-2 (lib. bdg.)   ISBN 0-8167-2922-0 (pbk.)
    1. Bailey, Pearl—Juvenile literature.   2. Singers—United States—
Biography—Juvenile literature.   [1. Bailey, Pearl.   2. Singers.
3. Afro-Americans—Biography.]   I. Griffith, Gershom, ill.
II. Title.
ML3930.B207B7   1993
782.42164´092—dc20
[B]   92-20190

Pearl Bailey

WITH A SONG IN HER HEART

It was Sunday morning in the Bailey house. The Reverend Joseph James Bailey stood at the open front door. "There is nothing worse than a preacher getting to church after his congregation," he said impatiently. "You kids get a move on!"

Virgie, Eura, and Willie came running down the stairs. "Good," Mr. Bailey said, "you all look neat and clean. But where's your little sister?"

"She's with me," Mrs. Bailey called from upstairs. "We'll be right with you."

A moment later, Ella Mae Bailey and her three-year-old daughter appeared. Mr. Bailey took one look at his youngest child and gasped. "What happened to my baby?" he asked.

The little girl grinned at him. "I went and got a haircut all by myself," she said proudly. "It's a good one, isn't it?"

Mrs. Bailey said, "Leave it to Pearlie Mae. She certainly knows how to be different. I sent her to the barber yesterday to get a regular haircut. And she came back looking like this! She told the barber to cut off all of her hair—and he did!"

Little Pearl's smile faded and tears began to form in her eyes. "That's all right," Mr. Bailey told her, taking her hand. "You're beautiful . . . even bald."

When Pearl Mae Bailey walked into church that morning, everyone looked at her. It was the first time in her life that she was the center of attention. But it certainly wasn't the last. This time, she was noticed for having no hair on her head. For the rest of her life, people admired her for her talent, warm personality, devotion to others, and her enthusiasm for learning. Almost from the day she was born, March 29, 1918, Pearl Bailey was a standout, a wonderful one-of-a-kind.

There was always something going on in the
Bailey house. Reverend Bailey tried out his
sermons on the family. He knew he had a good
one if his children paid close attention. To keep
them interested, he used humor and story-telling
to make the Bible come alive. The power of his
words impressed little Pearl deeply. And the
religious message became a permanent part of
her life.

Mrs. Bailey, a sweet, caring woman, also had a strong influence on her children. As Pearl Bailey remembered, her mother used "sugar" in her words, while Mr. Bailey used "salt"—but both were loving parents. And both were strict with their children, too.

While there was a lot of fun and laughter in the Bailey house, there were rules to follow. A preacher's children were expected to keep out of fights, to attend services regularly, and to show respect for everybody at all times. They were constantly reminded to be models of good behavior. The Bailey children tried their best to meet that standard.

In 1922, the family moved to Washington, D.C.
A few years later, Mr. and Mrs. Bailey separated.
The children lived with their mother, and Mr.
Bailey lived nearby. Pearl saw her father every
Sunday at church. He also visited during the
week. Sometimes Pearl wondered why her parents
were not together. One time her mother explained,
"Your father is a fine man. We respect each other
and we both care for you children. It's just that
we're different in too many ways."

Even though their parents were apart, the Bailey children led happy, ordinary lives. They went to school and had to show their homework and report cards to both parents. Mama gave her approval with smiles and laughter. When a mark wasn't good enough, she didn't say much. She didn't have to—her silence said plenty.

Papa was different. He never spanked his children. But his "work hard" lectures were as powerful as his sermons. Between the two parents, the children found it wisest to do well in school and avoid problems at home.

Sunday was always the busiest day of the week. It began with church services. Reverend Bailey's church, the House of Prayer, was an exciting place to be. The choir practiced all week and sang as well as any professional chorus. Singing and dancing were part of the worship, and everyone—young and old—joined in.

When she was an adult, Pearl Bailey always said that she learned harmony and rhythm at those joyous meetings. She pointed out that the music in African-American churches has had a powerful influence on all kinds of music: ragtime, jazz, blues, rock and roll . . . . "Just listen to the beat," she said, "and go to one of the churches and see if you don't hear the same thing."

Little Pearl never took a lesson in singing or dancing. She didn't need to. She sang and danced in church, and that was her musical education. Her talent was obvious, right from the beginning.

After church services, the children always took a drive with Papa in his open car. They drove around the neighborhood, greeting all the folks they knew. The children were expected to sit up straight and act properly. If they were good and didn't start fussing or fighting with each other, their reward was movie money.

Back then, a child's ticket at the local movie house cost ten cents. An extra penny or two bought candy or popcorn. In those days, movies were silent. A piano player in the theater played music to fit the action on the screen. There was fast "chase" music when the sheriff's posse rode after the bad guys. There was slow, sweet music for the kissing scenes. And there was sad music when an orphaned child was forced out into a storm.

Even though there was no sound, the audience understood what was happening. The screen was often filled with action. There were comedies with pies thrown, paint cans falling from ladders, people slipping on banana peels. Words sometimes flashed on the screen. They told what the people in the movie were saying, or explained what was going to happen next.

For Pearl, the best movies were the serials. These were stories that continued week after week. Each week's segment ended with the hero or heroine in terrible danger—hanging from a cliff, locked in a trunk at the bottom of the sea, falling from an airplane, trapped in a fiery building . . . . It seemed there was no escape. Then, the next week's segment began with a miracle rescue, followed by more action, and ending with yet another "certain death" scene.

Pearl looked forward to going to the movies. She knew what she was seeing wasn't real, but the feelings movies gave her *were* real. She laughed and cried, and saw that everyone around her had the same reactions. Like her father's sermons, Pearl realized, music and dance and movies were very powerful. They reached out and touched people deeply. This was something she never forgot.

As a performer, Pearl Bailey enjoyed making people laugh and cry and feel strong emotions. It made her happy to make her audiences happy. As she once said, "I love people; they can have everything I've got." And because she was warm and honest and outgoing, audiences loved her and always came back for more.

Being a star on the stage or in the movies was a long way from watching silent films in Washington, D.C. Back then, the idea of a show-business career was far from little Pearl's mind. What she wanted to be was a teacher.

In 1929, Ella Mae Bailey remarried and moved to Philadelphia, Pennsylvania. The Bailey children stayed with their father for a few months. Then Virgie got married, and soon after, the other three Bailey children went to live with their mother and stepfather, Walter Robinson.

In Philadelphia, Pearl attended the Joseph Singerly School, the John F. Reynolds School, and William Penn High School. She was a very good student and still planned to become a teacher. But Pearl's plans took a turn in a different direction when she was fifteen years old.

Her brother Willie, who was nineteen, was working as a tap dancer at a local theater. One night, their mother sent Pearl to the theater with a message for Willie. He was rehearsing when she got there, so she waited for him backstage. It was the first time Pearl had ever been backstage in a theater, and it fascinated her. She gawked at the scenery, the lights, the stagehands, the performers—everything and everyone.

When Willie came offstage, he took the message and told Pearl to go right home. He didn't want his baby sister hanging around. This "big-brother bossiness" bothered Pearl. Then she saw a sign that read "Amateur Night Tonight," and got an idea. She decided to enter the amateur night contest, just to embarrass her brother.

That night Pearl returned to the theater and asked the theater manager to let her perform. He knew she was Willie's little sister, so he agreed. When Pearl's turn came, she sang two songs and did a little tap dance. The audience clapped and whistled its approval, and Pearl Mae Bailey won the five-dollar first prize. With it came a week's work at the theater.

From that day on, Pearl was in love with show business. Now the teenager wasn't so sure she wanted to be a teacher. Being on the stage in front of a loving audience—that became her new ambition.

The next summer, during vacation, Pearl went to New York to visit Willie and his wife, Jessie Scott. They were a dance team, performing at a nightclub in the city. They took Pearl to see shows at different theaters, and they introduced her to their show-business friends.

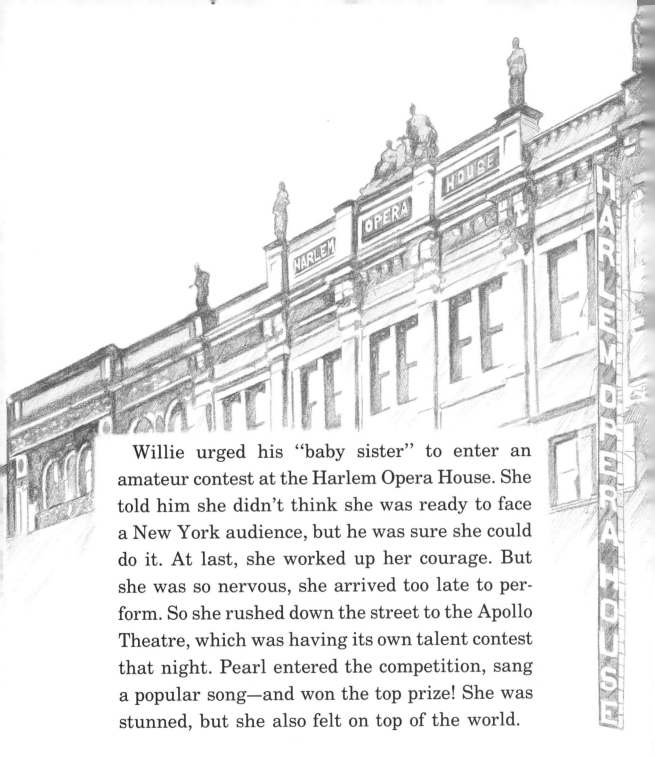

Willie urged his "baby sister" to enter an amateur contest at the Harlem Opera House. She told him she didn't think she was ready to face a New York audience, but he was sure she could do it. At last, she worked up her courage. But she was so nervous, she arrived too late to perform. So she rushed down the street to the Apollo Theatre, which was having its own talent contest that night. Pearl entered the competition, sang a popular song—and won the top prize! She was stunned, but she also felt on top of the world.

26

Years later, Pearl Bailey said that was one of her luckiest nights, for two reasons. First, she won the contest at the Apollo Theatre, one of the most famous theaters in the world.

Second, she missed the contest at the Harlem Opera House. That night at the Opera House an unknown singer named Ella Fitzgerald took first prize. She went on to become one of the finest popular singers of the twentieth century!

After that exciting summer, Pearl went back to
school in Philadelphia. Two years later, after she
finished high school, Pearl began her professional
career. She teamed up with a young male dancer
and they worked with a popular orchestra. Pearl
and her partner danced between the acts of the
shows. This gave the stagehands time to change
the scenery behind the curtain.

"We ended up in Indian costumes," Pearl Bailey later wrote, "doing a fast dance across the stage. Papa would have liked that. He was half Creek Indian."

That job was followed by a few weeks as a chorus girl in a New York theater. Pearl earned twenty-two dollars a week. It was enough to pay for her meals and rent. Then the job ended and nothing new turned up, so Pearl went back home to Philadelphia. There wasn't much work of any kind in those days. It was the time of the Great Depression. Lots of people were homeless and hungry. Pearl knew she was lucky to have a home and family to return to.

For the next few years the young singer-dancer worked in nightclubs and cities all over the eastern United States. It wasn't very glamorous work, but times were still hard and Pearl knew she was gaining valuable experience. Some weeks she was paid twelve or fifteen dollars, and some weeks she wasn't paid at all. In some towns room and board were free; in other places she had to pay for everything. Either way, she was just managing to survive.

One time, Pearl Bailey remembered, she earned fifteen dollars a week. She paid three dollars for rent, three dollars for meals, and seven dollars and fifty cents for clothes, make-up, and other expenses. And she sent one dollar and fifty cents home to Mama. Some weeks the young trouper earned extra money by being a hairdresser to other performers. She also cooked, sewed costumes, and did housecleaning.

Pearl Bailey was never too proud to do any honest job. When she was poor, she did it to support herself. When she was successful, she did her own work because it felt right. She always loved to cook and to see people enjoying her food.

In 1941, Pearl Bailey's musical career was just beginning to take off. Then World War Two started, and everything changed. A month later she joined a tour sponsored by the United Service Organizations. The USO put on shows at military bases throughout the United States and overseas. The entertainers helped to lift the spirits of men and women serving in the armed forces.

Pearl Bailey spent most of the war years working with the USO, taking brief breaks for nightclub appearances. Entertaining the troops made her feel good and gave her even more professional experience. As she later wrote, "The USO helped me a lot; those soldiers wanted lots of entertainment. You sang and talked and joked, so I really developed more talent than I dreamed of."

By the end of the war, in 1945, Pearl Bailey was famous. Soon after, she made her movie debut in *Variety Girl,* and appeared in a dozen other films. Her favorite role was in *Porgy and Bess.* Between movies, Pearl Bailey starred in a number of Broadway musicals, including *St. Louis Woman* and *House of Flowers.* Then, in 1967, she wowed audiences in her most famous role, Dolly in *Hello, Dolly!*

If audiences loved Pearl Bailey before, they adored her as the outgoing matchmaker, Dolly Levi. So did the critics. *The New York Times* review said, "For Miss Bailey this was a Broadway triumph for the history books . . . . The audience would have elected her governor if she'd only named her choice of state." The show's composer, Jerry Herman, said she was "absolutely sensational."

Nobody enjoyed the part she played more than Pearl Bailey herself. She said it was a fantastic emotional experience. "At last I can sing, dance, say intelligent words on stage, love and be loved, and deliver what God gave me—and I'm dressed up besides. I'm really Dolly."

Pearl Bailey loved to work, and she had an endless supply of energy. She sang in nightclubs and did concert tours. She appeared on television in her own show, and as a guest on soap operas, specials, fund-raising benefits, and dramatic plays. But the most enjoyable work of all, she said, was appearing with her husband, drummer Louis Bellson, and his orchestra.

Pearl Bailey and Louis Bellson made an ideal couple. They were two of the happiest, most gentle people in show business. In 1952, when Mr. Bellson was on his way to London, England, to marry Pearl Bailey, she was asked by reporters how they could recognize him at the airport. "The first person who gets off the plane smiling, that's Louis," she told them.

"After the plane landed," Pearl Bailey remembered, "there was a guy coming down the stairs, smiling as usual at the world." Of course, it was Louis Bellson.

Some people made prejudiced remarks about the marriage, because Pearl Bailey was black and Louis Bellson was white. When one of those remarks appeared in a newspaper, Pearl Bailey was asked how it made her feel. "This was my well-known reply," she later wrote. "There is only one race, the human race. The world, I hope, will never forget that one line, because I meant it."

Pearl Bailey also found time to write six books. In addition, she contributed many hours to public service groups, such as the March of Dimes and the USO. In 1975, President Gerald Ford appointed Pearl Bailey as Special Advisor to the U.S. Mission of the United Nations General Assembly. She remained in that post for the rest of her life.

In 1978, Georgetown University awarded Pearl Bailey an honorary doctorate for her humanitarian work. After the ceremony, she said to university officials, "This is certainly wonderful, but I wish I had a real degree." One of the officials answered, "That's no problem. Whenever you're ready, you come in. If you want to go to college, we'll help you in any way we can."

Pearl Bailey took him at his word. In 1979, when she was sixty-one years old, she entered the freshman class at Georgetown University. And she worked as hard at her studies as she did at everything else. Anytime a teacher recommended a book, Pearl Bailey wrote down the title. Then she went out, bought it, and read it. She loved to read, to do research, and to learn.

Pearl Bailey never felt that being a star made her better than anyone else. While she was at Georgetown, two of her young classmates asked a teacher how they could meet the famous performer. "Leave a note on her car," he told them. They did. The next day Pearl Bailey called the girls and invited them to her apartment. She was delighted to talk with her fellow students. Then she cooked dinner and served it to them. Onstage, Pearl Bailey was a star. Offstage, she was a warm, down-to-earth human being.

Pearl Bailey was also filled with school spirit. Once, at a Georgetown basketball game, she rushed onto the floor and joined the cheerleaders. She bounced around and led the cheers with the rest of the squad. The fans loved it. So did the sixty-five-year-old cheerleader, although, as she said when she was back in her seat, "Honey, I think I'm getting too old for this kind of thing."

When Pearl Bailey started college, she planned
to major in modern languages. But her reading
and the classes she took led her to a major in
theology instead. This was in keeping with her
lifelong interest in religion and her deep faith in
God. And it was another example of Pearl Bailey
doing things in her own unique way. There she
was, the daughter of an evangelical Protestant
minister, taking her degree at a Catholic university. And her special interest was Jewish
studies! In her school life, as in the rest of her
life, Pearl Bailey embraced the world.

In 1985, at the age of sixty-seven, Pearl Bailey received her Bachelor of Arts degree from Georgetown University. It was another glorious moment in a very full life. Pearl Bailey continued working and enjoying that life until her death on August 17, 1990. Right to the end, her heart was filled with music and love. And she blessed the world with both.

INDEX